M000235532

Sermon Outlines for Busy Pastors

Sermon Outlines for Busy Pastors

Russell Spray

BAKER BOOK HOUSE
Grand Rapids, Michigan 49516

Copyright © 1989 by Baker Books
a division of Baker Book House Company
P.O. Box 6287, Grand Rapids, MI 49516-6287

ISBN: 0-8010-8294-3

Sixth printing, October 1996

Printed in the United States of America

For information about academic books, resources for Christian
leaders, and all new releases available from Baker Book House
visit our web site:

http://www.bakerbooks.com

Contents

Foreword

Sermon Outlines for Busy Pastors is designed to assist ministers with their sermon preparation. The authors give direction and make the messages easy to remember.

May God bless all those who use and hear these *Sermon Outlines for Busy Pastors*.

Russell E. Spray

1

Dynamics of God's Love

"For God so loved the world, that he gave his only begotten Son, that whosoever believeth in him should not perish, but have everlasting life" (John 3:16).

The following points describe the greatness and goodness of God's love:

I. God's Love Is Plenteous

"God so loved the world . . ." (John 3:16).

A. Millions of people in our world lack food, clothing, and shelter. They are destitute as far as life's necessities are concerned.

B. There seems to be plenty for everyone in our country. However, many are homeless and some are starving to death.

C. It is comforting to know that there is no short supply of God's love. It is sufficient for all. "God so loved the world"—the small and great, rich and poor alike. No one is left out.

II. God's Love Is Priceless

". . . that he gave his only begotten Son . . ." (John 3:16).

A. Much of today's love is cheap and temporary. The divorce rate almost surpasses the number of marriages.

B. God's love is priceless. He gave His only Son to die for our sins. No one else could atone. God gave the best heaven had to offer because of His priceless love for us.

C. We deserve to die for our sins. "For the wages of sin is death; but the gift of God is eternal life through Jesus Christ our Lord" (Rom. 6:23).

III. God's Love Is Protective

". . . that whosoever believeth in him should not perish . . ."
(John 3:16).

A. The love of a mother and father is great. Parents strive to protect their children from harm and danger.

B. God's love is greater. We sinned and deserved to die, but God's protective love saved us from wrath. We must believe to receive.

C. Ours is a dangerous world. Terrorism is spreading death and destruction throughout the world. God watches over His own. "For he shall give his angels charge over thee . . ." (Ps. 91:11).

IV. God's Love Is Permanent

". . . but have everlasting life" (John 3:16).

A. Few things in today's world are permanent. Almost everything rusts, decays, is stolen, or destroyed.

B. It is uplifting to know that God's love is permanent. It does not last for just a day, week, month, or year. God's love is eternal. "God is love" (I John 4:8).

C. Christians can be filled with God's love. They can enjoy happiness in this life and everlasting life in the world to come.

2

Doing the W-I-L-L of God

"Make you perfect in every good work to do his will, working in you that which is well-pleasing in his sight, through Jesus Christ" (Heb. 13:21).

Christians should desire to do God's will. The following thoughts should help us reach that goal:

I. W-alk with the Lord

"And Enoch walked with God . . ." (Gen. 5:22).

A. Many Christians try to hold on to God with one hand and the world with the other hand.

B. God will not settle for just a part of us. We must surrender all to Him, withholding nothing.

C. To walk with the Lord, we must seek to please Him. We must partake of His Word and continue in a spirit of prayer at all times (I Thess. 5:17).

II. I-nvest in the Lord

"But lay up for yourselves treasures in heaven . . ." (Matt. 6:20).

A. Temporal pursuits come first with millions of people. They seek for real estate holdings, money market certificates, and stocks and bonds.

B. To do the will of God, we must give Him first place in our affections.

C. God's Word admonishes us to "seek ye first the kingdom of God, and his righteousness; and all these things shall be added unto you" (Matt. 6:33).

III. L-ook to the Lord

"Looking unto Jesus the author and finisher of our faith" (Heb. 12:2).

- A. Some Christians look to possessions, pleasure, power, and position more than to the Lord.
- B. To do God's will, we must keep our eyes on Jesus. He is the One who never fails.
- C. Promises fail. Money fails. Treasures fail. People fail. But Jesus never fails (Matt. 24:35).

IV. L-ove as the Lord

". . . the Son of God, who loved me, and gave himself for me" (Gal. 2:20).

- A. Many Christians are remiss when it comes to loving God and others. They are selfishly motivated.
- B. We must love the Lord with all our heart, soul, strength, and mind, and our neighbor as ourself (Luke 10:27).
- C. To do God's will we must walk with the Lord, invest in the Lord, look to the Lord, and love as the Lord.

3

"Even Our F-A-I-T-H"

"And this is the victory that overcometh the world, even our faith"
(I John 5:4).

The following points explain the value of faith and enumerate some of the things that it brings to believers:

I. Faith Brings F-reedom
"If the Son therefore shall make you free, ye shall be free indeed" (John 8:36).
- A. Some Christians are bound by false guilt. They are denied many of God's blessings because they suffer unnecessarily.
- B. We must recognize that which is false and then accept our freedom in Christ through faith. We are forgiven, cleansed, and promised heaven (Rom. 3:24).

II. Faith Brings A-ction
"But be ye doers of the word, and not hearers only ..." (James 1:22).
- A. Many Christians willingly talk about faith, but they stop there. Scripture tells us that "faith without works is dead" (James 2:20).
- B. To be effective, faith must be active. Our faith works for us only as we work our faith. Active faith requires doing, being, speaking, living, and loving God and others.

III. Faith Brings I-nsight
"If any of you lack wisdom, let him ask of God ... and it shall be given him" (James 1:5).
- A. Many Christians lack spiritual insight. They do or say things that hinder and hurt God's kingdom.

B. God wants to help His people make right choices and decisions. Wisdom is given to those who "ask in faith" (James 1:6).

IV. Faith Brings T-rust

"And the LORD shall help them, and deliver them . . . because they trust in him" (Ps. 37:40).

A. Many Christians fail to completely trust the Lord. They look to temporal things—houses, cars, and money for their security.

B. Faith brings trust. Trust causes one to rely or depend on, to commit to, or to have confidence in. We must trust in the Lord. He never fails (I John 5:14–15).

V. Faith Brings H-eaven

". . . believe also in me. In my Father's house are many mansions" (John 14:1–2).

A. Faith brings heaven. Jesus promised to prepare a place for those who believe in Him.

B. He also promised, "I will come again, and receive you unto myself; that where I am, there ye may be also" (John 14:3).

4

God's Gifts to His People

"Fear thou not; for I am with thee: be not dismayed; for I am thy God: I will strengthen thee; yea, I will help thee; yea, I will uphold thee with the right hand of my righteousness" (Isa. 41:10).

Let us look at some of God's gifts to His people:

I. He Gives Serenity
"Fear thou not; for I am with thee" (Isa. 41:10).
   A. Many Christians lack the peace that God wants them to have. They fail to accept His peace by faith.
   B. The assurance of God's presence brings peace. He promised, "I am with thee" (Isa. 41:10). Let us believe it. Receive God's peace today (John 14:27).

II. He Gives Security
"Be not dismayed; for I am thy God" (Isa. 41:10).
   A. Many people seek security by acquiring substantial bank accounts, stocks and bonds, real estate holdings, and cars, but still feel insecure.
   B. Security is not found in temporal accumulations, but in God who created the heavens and the earth. He said, "I am thy God"(Isa. 41:10). That's security (Phil. 4:19).

III. He Gives Strength
"I will strengthen thee" (Isa. 41:10).
   A. Many Christians fall short because they lack the strength to perform the tasks God has given them to do.
   B. We must accept by faith and with thanksgiving the strength God has promised to give us (Phil. 4:13).

IV. He Gives Stamina

"Yea, I will help thee" (Isa. 41:10).

A. Stamina means: "STAYING POWER, ENDURANCE"—Webster.

B. God didn't promise to do everything for us, but He did promise to help us through hardships. We must rely on His Word and believe that He is helping us now (Isa. 41:13).

V. He Gives Stability

"Yea, I will uphold thee with the right hand of my righteousness" (Isa. 41:10).

A. Many Christians are weak and unstable. They rely only on their own strength.

B. Stability comes from God. He has promised to "uphold thee with the right hand of my righteousness" (Isa. 41:10). We need to keep on praying, trusting, and obeying. God will do the rest. He is our great stabilizing force.

5

God's Enabling Power

"Strengthened with all might, according to his glorious power, unto all patience and longsuffering with joyfulness" (Col. 1:11).

Christians need not solely depend on their own strength. God's omnipotent power is available to them. He can enable them . . .

I. To Be Patient

". . . unto all patience . . ." (Col. 1:11).

A. Many Christians lack patience. They want things to happen in their own appointed time and way. They fail to be the blessing they should be.

B. We must wait on the Lord, accept His timing and mode of answering our prayers. His timing and methods are always right.

C. We should be patient with ourselves and others too. The scriptures admonish, "in your patience possess ye your souls" (Luke 21:19).

II. To Be Persevering

". . . and longsuffering . . ." (Col. 1:11).

A. Many Christians give up too quickly. When the going gets rough, they throw up their hands in despair. They fail to keep on keeping on.

B. Persevere means: "to persist in a state, enterprise, or undertaking in spite of counter influences, opposition, or discouragement"—Webster.

C. God has a purpose in what He allows us to endure. He promised, "After that ye have suffered a while, make you perfect, stablish, strengthen, settle you" (I Peter 5:10).

III. To Give Praise

". . . with joyfulness" (Col. 1:11).

A. Many Christians do not rejoice in the Lord sufficiently. They wear sad expressions and possess a negative attitude.

B. Paul admonished Christians to "rejoice in the Lord always: and again I say, Rejoice" (Phil. 4:4).

C. Praising brings rejoicing. The psalmist said, "From the rising of the sun unto the going down of the same the LORD's name is to be praised" (Ps. 113:3). Let us praise Him joyfully.

6

Giving Thanks to God

"And whatsoever ye do in word or deed, do all in the name of the Lord Jesus, giving thanks to God and the Father by him" (Col. 3:17).

I. Thank Him IN Everything

"In every thing give thanks: for this is the will of God in Christ Jesus concerning you" (I Thess. 5:18).

A. Many people thank God in good times but fail to thank Him when the going gets rough.

B. Some Christians are selfishly motivated. They put their own desires ahead of God's. We must give Him first place (Matt. 6:33).

C. We should seek God's will and heed Paul's advice: "In every thing give thanks: for this is the will of God . . ." (I Thess. 5:18).

II. Thank Him FOR Everything

"Giving thanks always for all things unto God . . ." (Eph. 5:20).

A. Many Christians are ready to thank God for the good but not the bad things that happen to them.

B. God may not send the bad, but He sometimes allows it to come to fulfill His purpose.

C. We should thank God for all things, knowing that He works everything together for our good and His glory (Rom. 8:28).

III. Thank Him WITH Everything

"Praise him with the sound of the trumpet. . . . Let everything that hath breath praise the LORD . . ." (Ps. 150:3, 6).

A. People often do not thank God with everything. They withhold a part for themselves.

B. We must show our thanks to God by putting everything we are and own at His disposal, including our time, talent, and treasure.

C. The more we give, the more He will supply, for if we give, the more He will do for us (Luke 6:38).

IV. Thank Him THROUGH Everything

"If any man suffer as a Christian . . . let him glorify God on this behalf" (I Peter 4:16).

A. Some Christians thank God while going through mountain-top experiences but fail to thank Him while traversing the valleys.

B. God allows testing, trial, and temptation to expand our faith and take us deeper in His love.

C. "Concerning the fiery trial," Peter advised, "But rejoice, inasmuch as ye are partakers of Christ's sufferings; that, when his glory shall be revealed, ye may be glad also with exceeding joy" (I Peter 4:12–13).

7

How to Be Conquerors

"Nay, in all these things we are more than conquerors through him that loved us" (Rom. 8:37).

Too many Christians fail in their quest for a victorious life. The following points tell us how to win:

I. Prevail in Prayer to God
". . . men ought always to pray, and not to faint" (Luke 18:1).
- A. Prevail means: "TRIUMPH . . . to be or become effective . . . PERSIST"—Webster.
- B. Many Christians fail in prayer because of neglect. They settle for just a "Now I lay me down to sleep" type of prayer.
- C. To win in prayer we must pray with sincerity and perseverance. We can be conquerors in prayer.

II. Pursue the Promises of God
"For whatsoever things were written aforetime were written for our learning . . ." (Rom. 15:4).
- A. Some people may think the promises of God were written for the patriarchs but not for present-day Christians.
- B. God's Word teaches they "were written for our learning, that we through patience and comfort of the scriptures might have hope" (Rom. 15:4).
- C. Let us seek out the promises which fit our area of need, read them, claim them as our own, and recall them often. We can conquer through God's Word.

III. Practice the Presence of God
"Draw nigh to God, and he will draw nigh to you" (James 4:8).
- A. Drawing near to God comes through the recognition and

awareness of God's presence as being with us at all times. He promised, "I will never leave thee, nor forsake thee" (Heb. 13:5).

B. We practice God's presence when we pray, read God's Word, and worship Him in spirit and truth.

C. We also practice the presence of God while participating in His work. Doing God's work draws us closer to Him.

IV. Proclaim the Praises of God

"While I live will I praise the LORD" (Ps. 146:2).

A. Some Christians fail to live victoriously because they do not praise the Lord enough.

B. The psalmist said, "I will sing praises unto my God while I have any being" (Ps. 146:2).

C. We can be conquerors by proclaiming the praises of God as the psalmist did (Ps. 145:2–3).

8

How Christians Should Think

"Let this mind be in you, which was also in Christ Jesus" (Phil. 2:5).

Christians need to guard their thought life. Let us look at some ways we can do that:

I. Think Pure Thoughts
"...whatsoever things are pure...think on these things" (Phil. 4:8).
- A. Many Christians allow themselves to indulge in impure thoughts.
- B. In his determination to defeat God's purpose, Satan bombards Christian minds with impure thoughts.
- C. We must be on the alert and with deliberate action, replace impure thoughts with pure ones. With practice this becomes easier to accomplish.

II. Think Positive Thoughts
"... whatsoever things are of good report ... think on these things" (Phil. 4:8).
- A. Millions of Christians wrestle with negative thinking. Negativism is defeating.
- B. We need not be overcome. With God's help we can replace negative thoughts with positive assertions.
- C. When pessimistic thoughts come, by an act of the will, we should deliberately turn from them by looking for the good and not the bad.

III. Think Peaceful Thoughts
"And let the peace of God rule in your hearts ..." (Col. 3:15).

A. Evil and destructive forces have captured the imagination of our society. There remains little or no peace and quiet.
B. Through prayer, praise, and trust in God, Christians can think peaceful thoughts.
C. The promise is, "And the peace of God, which passeth all understanding, shall keep your hearts and minds through Christ Jesus" (Phil. 4:7).

IV. Think Purposeful Thoughts

"According to the eternal purpose which he purposed in Christ Jesus our Lord" (Eph. 3:11).

A. Many people live with little or no purpose. They simply exist from day to day.
B. God has a definite purpose for each of us. We must seek His guidance for our lives.
C. Christ lived with purpose, so must we. If we seek and accomplish God's purpose in this life, we will live eternally in the next.

9

How to Please the Lord

"That ye might walk worthy of the Lord unto all pleasing, being fruitful in every good work, and increasing in the knowledge of God" (Col. 1:10).

Let us consider some of the scriptural ways to please God:

I. The Walking

"That ye might walk worthy of the Lord unto all pleasing . . ." (Col. 1:10).

A. Many people profess to be Christians but do not "walk worthy of the Lord unto all pleasing" (Col. 1:10). They go their own way and do their own choosing.

B. Someone has said, "What you do speaks so loudly that I cannot hear what you say." We need to practice what we claim.

C. We must strive to follow Christ's example in our daily walk, giving Him first place, seeking to do those things pleasing in His sight (I John 3:22).

II. The Working

". . . being fruitful in every good work . . ." (Col. 1:10).

A. Some Christians are remiss when it comes to participating in God's work. They fail to get involved because they are too busily engaged in personal pursuits.

B. Some are not "fruitful in every good work" (Col. 1:10). They do their good works for selfish reasons and for personal honor and gain.

C. To please God we must work diligently for His kingdom, doing all for His glory. ". . . whatsoever ye do, do all to the glory of God" (I Cor. 10:31).

III. The Wisdom

". . . and increasing in the knowledge of God" (Col. 1:10).

A. Many Christians lack knowledge and wisdom about the things of God. Therefore, they fail to make the spiritual progress they could and should.

B. We obtain wisdom by "increasing in the knowledge of God" (Col. 1:10). We do this through the knowledge of the scriptures, by study and assimilation of His Word.

C. To please God we must search the scriptures, find the portions that fit our area of need. Wisdom is promised to those who ask and believe (James 1:5–6).

10

"I Must Tell Jesus"

"Casting all your care upon him; for he careth for you" (I Peter 5:7).

"I must tell Jesus!/I must tell Jesus!/I cannot bear my burdens alone;/I must tell Jesus!/I must tell Jesus;/Jesus can help me,/Jesus alone"—Refrain of the hymn, *I Must Tell Jesus.*

I. Tell Jesus Your Trials

"I must tell Jesus all of my trials;/I cannot bear these burdens alone./In my distress He kindly will help me;/He ever loves and cares for His own"—First verse of the hymn, I Must Tell Jesus.

A. All Christians must expect trials. God allows trials to strengthen us and deepen our faith (I Peter 1:7).

B. The scriptures admonish, "Beloved, think it not strange concerning the fiery trial which is to try you . . ." (I Peter 4:12).

C. God has a purpose in what He allows to come to us. He will deliver and keep those who come to Him (I Peter 1:5).

II. Tell Jesus Your Troubles

"I must tell Jesus all of my troubles;/He is a kind, compassionate Friend./If I but ask Him, He will deliver,/Make of my troubles quickly an end"—Second verse of the hymn, I Must Tell Jesus.

A. Today's world is filled with troubled people—on the job, in the marketplace, in the home. Christians are not exempt from woes.

B. Many people take their troubles to doctors, lawyers, or friends, but fail to get lasting relief.

C. Jesus said, "Come unto me, all ye that labour and are heavy laden, and I will give you rest" (Matt. 11:28). Jesus brings real and lasting help.

III. Tell Jesus Your Temptations

"Tempted and tried, I need a great Savior,/One who can help my burdens to bear./I must tell Jesus, I must tell Jesus;/He all my cares and sorrows will share"—Third verse of the hymn, I Must Tell Jesus.

- A. Jesus is "touched with the feeling of our infirmities." He "was in all points tempted like as we are, yet without sin" (Heb. 4:15).
- B. Jesus knows about our temptations. He cares and understands (Heb. 2:18).

11

Jesus the O-N-L-Y Way

"Jesus saith unto him, I am the way, the truth, and the life: no man cometh unto the Father, but by me" (John 14:6).

Millions of people are trying to get to heaven without Jesus Christ, but He is the *only* way we may be saved. It is the . . .

I. O-bedient Way

". . . he . . . became obedient unto death, even the death of the cross" (Phil. 2:8).

A. Humankind disobeyed God and came under the penalty of death. Jesus took our place, dying on the cross in our stead.

B. Many people disobey God today. They are set in their ways and refuse to give up their sins.

C. To be saved we must obey the call of God. We must confess and forsake our sins, and believe on the Lord Jesus Christ (I John 1:9).

II. N-ecessary Way

"For there is none other name under heaven given among men, whereby we must be saved" (Acts 4:12).

A. Millions of people are leaving Jesus Christ out of their lives, yet they hope to make it to heaven.

B. They will come to disappointment, for Jesus is the only way. "Neither is there salvation in any other" (Acts 4:12).

C. The scriptures teach, "That at the name of Jesus every knee should bow . . . And that every tongue should confess that Jesus Christ is Lord . . ." (Phil. 2:10–11).

III. L-oving Way

"... as Christ also hath loved us, and hath given himself for us ..." (Eph. 5:2).

A. God loved us so much that He gave His Son Jesus to become the propitiation for the sins of mankind (I John 4:10).

B. Jesus loved us and gave Himself to die on the cross for us. He freely took our sins upon Himself (I John 2:2).

C. We must love the Lord and others too. Our love grows as we do those things pleasing to Him and "walk, even as he walked" (I John 2:6).

IV. Y-ielded Way

"Nevertheless not my will, but thine, be done" (Luke 22:42).

A. In His most excruciating hour, Jesus yielded His will to His heavenly Father's will.

B. We must yield our will to God's will also. Some people hold on to certain pleasures and possessions for selfish reasons.

C. God requires total surrender and a yielded will. He accepts nothing less. We should pray as Jesus did, "Not my will, but thine, be done."

12

Let His Spirit L-I-F-T You

"That he would grant you, according to the riches of his glory, to be strengthened with might by his Spirit in the inner man" (Eph. 3:16).

The following points should assist Christians in their spiritual growth and progress:

I. L-earn

"... the Holy Ghost ... shall teach you all things ..." (John 14:26).

A. Many Christians are obstinate. They have difficulty learning from God. They also fail to learn from others.

B. The Lord teaches those who are willing to learn. He promised, "I will instruct thee and teach thee in the way which thou shalt go" (Ps. 32:8).

C. The Holy Spirit lifts those who are willing to be taught by Him. They are blessed and are a blessing to others.

II. I-nvest

"Set your affection on things above, not on things on the earth" (Col. 3:2).

A. If we are to be lifted by the Spirit of God, we must invest our time, talent, and treasure wisely.

B. We must take time for God's Word and prayer. We must use our abilities for God as opportunity affords.

C. We should pay tithe on our income and be generous with our offerings, helping to build God's kingdom (Matt. 6:20–21).

III. F-ollow

". . . the Spirit of truth . . . will guide you into all truth" (John 16:13).

A. Many Christians get ahead of the Lord. Disregarding Him, they go their own way and end up floundering and failing.

B. Some people follow another person instead of the Lord. They come to frustration and confusion.

C. We must follow the Lord. His Spirit lifts, guides, and directs those who follow faithfully.

IV. T-rust

"Commit thy way unto the LORD; trust also in him . . ." (Ps. 37:5).

A. Some Christians refuse to commit everything to God. They hold on to something for themselves.

B. If we are to be lifted by God's Spirit, we must be totally committed to His will (Rom. 12:1).

C. God's Spirit lifts those who learn from Him, invest in eternal values, follow in Christ's steps, and trust the Lord implicitly.

13

Let Christ Be Lord

Scripture Reading: Philippians 2:5–11
"And that every tongue should confess that Jesus Christ is Lord, to the glory of God the Father" (Phil. 2:11).

I. Lord of Your Thinking

"Let this mind be in you, which was also in Christ Jesus" (Phil. 2:5).

A. Some Christians fail because they let negative thoughts rule their thinking.

B. We must deliberately replace negative thoughts with positive ones. When we do, the Holy Spirit will help us to keep an optimistic outlook.

II. Lord of Your Hearing

"Incline your ear ... hear, and your soul shall live" (Isa. 55:3).

A. Too many Christians incline their ears to the lewdness and violence on the airways. Their spirit is dwarfed.

B. We must listen to the goodness of the Lord. He often speaks in a "still small voice."

III. Lord of Your Seeing

"Looking unto Jesus the author and finisher of our faith" (Heb. 12:2).

A. Some Christians look for the bad in others. They see only faults and failures.

B. We must look for the good by keeping our eyes on Jesus. Let Him be Lord of all our seeing.

IV. Lord of Your Talking

"For it is not ye that speak, but the Spirit of your Father which speaketh in you" (Matt. 10:20).

  A. Many Christians talk about almost everything except the Lord.

  B. We should talk about the things of the Lord—faith, hope, love, and the many miracles He performs.

V. Lord of Your Doing

". . . in every good work to do his will . . ." (Heb. 13:21).

  A. Many Christians falter when it comes to doing God's work. They are unconcerned or too busy with their own affairs.

  B. We must take time for God—attend church, give smiles and kind words, do good deeds, and witness to the unsaved as opportunity affords.

VI. Lord of Your Going

"As ye have therefore received Christ Jesus the Lord, so walk ye in him" (Col. 2:6).

  A. Millions of people are on the go searching for pleasure and pursuing personal interests.

  B. If we "walk in Him," He will go with us everywhere. We will find lasting joy and reap eternal rewards.

14

Make the Most of Y-O-U-R Life

"For what is your life? It is even a vapour, that appeareth for a little time, and then vanisheth away" (James 4:14).

Make the most of Y-O-U-R life. The following points tell us how:

I. Y-ield

". . . but yield yourselves unto the LORD . . ." (II Chron. 30:8).

A. Many Christians fail to yield themselves completely to God. They hold in reserve a portion of their life for selfish pursuits.

B. To make the most of our lives, we must yield all to God. We must give Him first place in every facet of life (Matt. 6:33).

II. O-bey

". . . obeying the truth through the Spirit unto unfeigned love of the brethren . . ." (I Peter 1:22).

A. Some Christians are not wholly obedient. They lack in love for God and fellow Christians.

B. To make the most of our life, we must obey the Lord implicitly. We must love God wholeheartedly and others also. We grow spiritually by "obeying the truth through the Spirit" (I Peter 1:22).

III. U-nite

"Endeavouring to keep the unity of the Spirit in the bond of peace" (Eph. 4:3).

A. Some people are disagreeable. They fail to live in harmony with their families and with other Christians. They make trouble for themselves and others.

B. We must live in unity with others. We must strive to "live peaceably with all men" (Rom. 12:18).

IV. R-ejoice

"Rejoice in the Lord always: and again I say, Rejoice" (Phil. 4:4).

A. Many Christians do not rejoice as much as they should. They wear long faces and possess negative attitudes. They fail to live triumphantly.

B. To make the most of our lives, we must rejoice in the Lord. The more we praise the Lord and exude a positive influence, the greater blessing we become and the more of God's blessings we receive.

15

Progressive Christians

Scripture Reading: I Corinthians 13
"And now abideth faith, hope, charity [love], these three; but the greatest of these is charity [love]" (I Cor. 13:13).

Christians cannot stand still. They must make progress.

I. Grow Upwardly by Faith
"And now abideth faith . . ." (I Cor. 13:13).

A. Some Christians fail to make spiritual progress. They continue to live in the lowlands of doubts and fears.

B. To please God we must "be no more children, tossed to and fro" (Eph. 4:14).

C. We must become established in the faith and "grow up into him in all things" (Eph. 4:15).

D. Spiritual progress and maturity come through prayer, study of God's Word, and doing those things that are pleasing to God (Heb. 11:6).

II. Glow Inwardly with Hope
"And now abideth . . . hope . . ." (I Cor. 13:13).

A. Millions of people are without hope in Christ. The rise in the suicide rate bears this out.

B. Christians glow inwardly with hope. ". . . God . . . hath given us everlasting consolation and good hope through grace" (II Thess. 2:16).

C. The hope that Christians have extends also to the life which is to come.

D. "Looking for that blessed hope, and the glorious appearing of the great God and our Savior Jesus Christ" (Titus 2:13).

III. Flow Outwardly with Love

"And now abideth . . . charity [love] . . ." (I Cor. 13:13).

A. Many Christians profess to love God but fail to love their fellowmen as they should.

B. We cannot truly love God unless we love others. ". . . he that loveth not his brother . . . how can he love God . . ."(I John 4:20).

C. Christians must flow outwardly with love. They should give a smile, a kind word, do a good deed, and witness to the lost as opportunity affords.

D. Let us be progressive Christians and flow outwardly with love. "And now abideth faith, hope, charity [love] . . . but the greatest of these is charity [love]" (I Cor. 13:13).

16

Praise the L-O-R-D

". . . let us offer the sacrifice of praise to God continually, that is, the fruit of our lips giving thanks to his name" (Heb. 13:15).

Christians can offer praise to God in the following ways:

I. L-ove the Lord

". . . Thou shalt love the Lord thy God with all thy heart . . . soul . . . strength . . . mind" (Luke 10:27).

A. Millions of people are involved in seeking temporal pursuits. They love material possessions more than they love God.

B. Many are thankless and self-centered. They profess to love God but seldom praise Him.

C. To truly love God, we must praise Him, giving Him first place in our lives.

II. O-bey the Lord

"Make you perfect in every good work to do his will . . ." (Heb. 13:21).

A. It is one thing to know God's will but another to do His will. We must obey Him "in every good work to do his will" (Heb. 13:21).

B. Many Christians try to please other people rather than to obey God. Their motives are selfish.

III. R-ejoice in the Lord

"Be glad in the LORD, and rejoice, ye righteous: and shout for joy . . ." (Ps. 32:11).

A. Many Christians fail to rejoice in the Lord as they should. They take themselves too seriously.

B. Some Christians are negative. They see all the bad things and miss the good things.
C. Praising the Lord will help us to be glad and rejoice in Him.

IV. D-epend on the Lord

"Trust in the LORD with all thine heart; and lean not unto thine own understanding" (Prov. 3:5).

A. Many Christians do not completely trust in the Lord. They depend on their own poor powers and fail.
B. Many depend on other people—doctors, lawyers, friends. Others depend on money, houses, cars, lands.
C. We must depend on God more than on anything or anyone else. To truly depend on Him, we must praise Him.

17

Resist the Devil

"Submit yourselves therefore to God. Resist the devil, and he will flee from you" (James 4:7).

The following points show us how to resist the devil:

I. Resist with Prayer

". . . men ought always to pray, and not to faint" (Luke 18:1).

A. Satan defeats Christians because they neglect to pray. Paul admonished Christians to "pray without ceasing" (I Thess. 5:17).

B. Prayer brings victories and produces miracles. It is the Christian's powerline to heaven (Matt. 21:22).

C. Christians should continue in a spirit of prayer at all times. Prayer defeats the devil.

II. Resist with the Promises

"Whereby are given unto us exceeding great and precious promises" (II Peter 1:4).

A. When Jesus was tempted, He used the Word of God to defeat the devil (Luke 4:1–13). We should follow His example.

B. After selecting the promises that fit the areas of our need, we should dwell on them, memorize them, and claim them as our own.

C. We resist the devil by claiming the promises of God. When we resist the devil, the promise is "he will flee from you" (James 4:7).

III. Resist with Perseverance

"But rejoice, inasmuch as ye are partakers of Christ's sufferings" (I Peter 4:13).

A. Perseverance means: "the action or condition or an instance of persevering: STEADFASTNESS"—Webster.

B. Many Christians falter and fail because they do not continue with patient and persistent effort.

C. We must never give up. We must keep on keeping on. We can resist the devil with perseverance (II Tim. 2:3).

IV. Resist with Praise

"From the rising of the sun unto the going down of the same the LORD's name is to be praised" (Ps. 113:3).

A. Most Christians do not praise the Lord enough. They are less than victorious.

B. Some Christians neglect to praise the Lord because they are too involved with temporal pursuits.

C. We must take time for God. When we praise the Lord, we resist the devil and receive the victory (Ps. 146:2).

18

Say "Yes" to God's Will

"And the world passeth away, and the lust thereof: but he that doeth the will of God abideth for ever" (I John 2:17).

Christians need to know and do God's will. The following points should offer help:

I. The *Who* of God's Will

"The Lord is . . . not willing that any should perish, but that all should come to repentance" (II Peter 3:9).

A. The "who" of God's will are the "whosoever wills." Everyone is included—all can be saved (John 3:16).

B. We must confess and forsake our sins, repent, believe, and accept Christ as Savior and Lord.

II. The *What* of God's Will

". . . but understanding what the will of the Lord is" (Eph. 5:17).

A. Devoted Christians want to know God's will for their lives.

B. To know what God's will is for us, we must pray, believe, and claim God's promises. ". . . if we ask any thing according to his will, he heareth us" (I John 5:14). "Make you perfect in every good work to do his will . . ." (Heb. 13:21).

III. The *Where* of God's Will

"I will . . . that men pray every where . . ." (I Tim. 2:8).

A. Christians should be in a spirit of prayer at all times.

B. We should pray at home, school, work, and even play. It is God's will that we "pray every where" (I Tim. 2:8).

IV. The *When* of God's Will

"Having made known unto us the mystery of his will, according to his good pleasure . . ." (Eph. 1:9).

A. Many Christians want God's will but insist that it be performed at their appointed time.

B. We must wait on the Lord and depend on His timing. He knows best. It is "according to his good pleasure" (Eph. 1:9).

V. The *Why* of God's Will

"For it is better, if the will of God be so, that ye suffer for well doing, than for evil doing" (I Peter 3:17).

A. The "why" of God's will can be the most difficult. We do not always understand the reason God allows some things to come into our lives.

B. We must wait in faith and know that God knows best. Everything that happens to us has first been screened by God's love (Rom. 8:28).

19

The Holy Spirit Gives Direction

"Howbeit when he, the Spirit of truth, is come, he will guide you into all truth" (John 16:13).

Christians need the daily direction of the Holy Spirit. He . . .

I. Directs Our Thinking
". . . whatsoever things are of good report . . . think on these things" (Phil. 4:8).
- A. Many Christians fail to let the Holy Spirit direct their thought life. They dwell on the negative and impure.
- B. With deliberate action we must replace negative with positive and unholy with holy thoughts. The Holy Spirit will help us to do so.

II. Directs Our Seeing
"Looking unto Jesus the author and finisher of our faith" (Heb. 12:2).
- A. Some Christians look for the bad instead of the good. They see only faults and failures.
- B. Sin and evil prevail in our society. The Holy Spirit directs those who look for the good.

III. Directs Our Hearing
"Incline your ear . . . hear, and your soul shall live" (Isa. 55:3).
- A. Foul language, lewdness, and lust dominate the airways of today's world.
- B. The Holy Spirit directs those who incline their ears to God's Word, will, and way.

IV. Directs Our Speaking

"For it is not ye that speak, but the Spirit of your Father which speaketh in you" (Matt. 10:20).

A. Christians must constantly guard their speech lest they speak harshly and unkindly.

B. We must depend on the direction of the Holy Spirit to give us the right words at the right time and place.

V. Directs Our Doing

"Labour . . . for that meat which endureth unto everlasting life . . ." (John 6:27).

A. Millions of people are busy with selfish interests and fail to do God's work as they should.

B. We must give God first place. We must let the Holy Spirit direct our labors.

VI. Directs Our Going

"As ye have therefore received Christ Jesus the Lord, so walk ye in him" (Col. 2:6).

A. Many Christians go to the wrong places in their search for entertainment. They leave God out of their activities.

B. We must seek the direction of the Holy Spirit. He will help us find real and lasting joy and contentment when we go with Him.

20

The Lord Is A-B-L-E

". . . he is able to keep that which I have committed unto him against that day" (II Tim. 1:12).

Listed below are some ways the Lord is able to help His own:

I. A-bundantly Able

"Now unto him that is able to do exceeding abundantly above all that we ask or think . . ." (Eph. 3:20).

A. Abundant means: "marked by great plenty; amply supplied: ABOUNDING; occurring in abundance: AMPLE"—Webster.

B. Many Christians depend on their own strength. They fail to trust God sufficiently.

C. We must depend on the Lord daily. He is abundantly able to fortify us against the stresses of life (Phil. 4:13).

II. B-ountifully Able

"And God is able to make all grace abound toward you . . ." (II Cor. 9:8).

A. Bountiful means: "liberal in bestowing gifts or favors; given or provided abundantly"—Webster.

B. Many people are tightfisted with God and others. They want to keep everything for themselves.

C. We cannot outgive the Lord. We must be generous with Him and others. The Lord is bountifully able to supply all our needs (Phil. 4:19).

III. L-ovingly Able

"Wherefore he is able also to save them to the uttermost that come unto God by him . . ." (Heb. 7:25).

A. Loving means: "AFFECTIONATE"—Webster.

B. God loved us so much that He gave His only Son Jesus Christ to die on the cross for our sins (John 3:16).

C. To be saved we must come to God in repentance and faith, accepting the Lord Jesus Christ.

IV. E-ternally Able

"Jesus Christ the same yesterday, and today, and for ever" (Heb. 13:8).

A. Eternal means: "having infinite duration: EVERLASTING . . . PERPETUAL . . ."—Webster.

B. Many people are changeable—here today and gone tomorrow. You never know where to find them.

C. The Lord never leaves nor forsakes His own. He is eternally able to stand by us and sustain us (Ps. 55:22).

21

The Reach of Faith

"Let us hold fast the profession of our faith without wavering; (for he is faithful that promised)" (Heb. 10:23).

To be effective, the Christian must have a faith that reaches into every direction.

I. Faith Reaches Upward
"Set your affection on things above, not on things on the earth" (Col. 3:2).
  A. The faith of some Christians does not reach very high. They are overwhelmed by the trials and cares of this life. They live beneath their privilege.
  B. True faith reaches upward into the heavens, beyond the highest star, the moon, and the sun. Faith reaches all the way up to God and transforms lives here on earth (Ps. 121:1–2).

II. Faith Reaches Downward
"But Jesus took him by the hand, and lifted him up" (Mark 9:27).
  A. Many Christians are shallow and complacent. They fail to accomplish God's work as they should. Their pride stymies their reach of faith.
  B. Real faith reaches downward to the lowest of the low, into the gutter of despair. It lifts the drunkard, prostitute, and homosexual—all those who are willing to repent and give up their sins (II Cor. 5:17).

III. Faith Reaches Inward
"Rooted and built up in him, and stablished in the faith ..." (Col. 2:7).

A. Some Christians are unstable. They lack faith in God and themselves. They flounder in their attempt to live a successful Christian life.
B. Faith reaches into the heart and soul to stabilize, establish, and enrich. It revives and renews the innermost parts of the soul. Faith is the victory (I John 5:4).

IV. Faith Reaches Outward

"Now faith is the substance of things hoped for, the evidence of things not seen" (Heb. 11:1).

A. The faith of many is confined to selfish motives and pursuits. It fails to reach outward to the poor, needy, and sinful of this world.
B. Through prayer, the promises, and generous giving, our faith can reach upward, downward, inward, and outward to the far corners of the world (Mark 16:15).

22

The Lord G-U-I-D-E-S His People

"When he, the Spirit of truth, is come, he will guide you into all truth" (John 16:13).

The Lord G-U-I-D-E-S His people in the following ways:

I. G-oes with His People
"...for the LORD thy God is with thee withersoever thou goest" (Josh. 1:9).
- A. As they travel the journey of life, some Christians fail to recognize the presence of God as they should.
- B. God is always with His people. He promised, "I will never leave thee, nor forsake thee" (Heb. 13:5).

II. U-nites His People
"Be of the same mind one toward another" (Rom. 12:16).
- A. Many Christians do not live in harmony. They are at odds with one another.
- B. While we may not always agree with others, we can disagree in an agreeable way (Rom. 12:18).

III. I-nstructs His People
"I will instruct thee and teach thee in the way which thou shalt go" (Ps. 32:8).
- A. The Lord instructs His people when they ask for it.
- B. We get His instructions through prayer, the promises, and by praising the Lord (Prov. 23:12).

IV. D-irects His People
"In all thy ways acknowledge him, and he shall direct thy paths" (Prov. 3:6).

A. Many Christians lose their way because they do not depend on the Lord to direct them.

B. We must give God first place and trust Him to order our steps (Ps. 37:23).

V. E-mpowers His People

"But ye shall receive power, after that the Holy Ghost is come upon you" (Acts 1:8).

A. Many Christians lack power for service. Their witness is weak and ineffective.

B. To receive the Holy Spirit's power, we first must make a total commitment to God, surrendering all to Him (Rom. 12:1–2).

VI. S-ustains His People

"... he is able to keep that which I have committed unto him..." (II Tim. 1:12).

A. The Holy Spirit sustains those who are completely yielded to Him. "... he will guide you into all truth ... he will show you things to come" (John 16:13).

B. The Lord goes with His people, unites His people, instructs His people, directs His people, empowers His people, and sustains His people.

23

The Heavenly Way

"And an highway shall be there, and a way, and it shall be called The way of holiness" (Isa. 35:8).

The heavenly way is . . .

I. A Pure Way
"The unclean shall not pass over it" (Isa. 35:8).
A. Millions of people travel the low road of sin and self-seeking. These lead to death and hell. God's highway of purity and holiness leads to eternal life and heaven.
B. The heavenly way is the way of purity and love. Jesus said, "Blessed are the pure in heart: for they shall see God" (Matt. 5:8).
C. When we totally commit our life to God, the Holy Spirit cleanses our heart and fills us with God's love. We are empowered for service as we travel the heavenly way.

II. A Protected Way
"No lion shall be there, nor any ravenous beast shall go up thereon . . ." (Isa. 35:9).
A. Ours is a dangerous world. Lust, greed, and destruction prevail without restraint. Many homes are invaded by separation and divorce.
B. The scriptures admonish, "Be sober, be vigilant; because your adversary the devil, as a roaring lion, walketh about, seeking whom he may devour" (I Peter 5:8).
C. There is no place of safety outside of Christ. We must depend on Him daily for protection. Satan cannot defeat those who trust in the Lord (Rom. 8:37).

III. A Pleasurable Way

"And the ransomed of the LORD shall return, and come to Zion with songs of everlasting joy upon their heads" (Isa. 35:10).

A. We live in a pleasure-mad society. Millions of people are trying to satisfy the longing in their souls with pleasure.

B. Sinful pleasures bring disappointment. "For the wages of sin is death; but the gift of God is eternal life through Jesus Christ our Lord" (Rom. 6:23).

C. The heavenly way is a pleasurable way. Totally committed Christians are forgiven and cleansed and on their way to heaven. Christ is not a disappointment. He never fails.

24

The Lord L-E-A-D-S His Own

"I will instruct thee and teach thee in the way which thou shalt go: I will guide thee with mine eye" (Ps. 32:8).

As God L-E-A-D-S His people, He . . .

I. L-oves His Own

". . . thou hast sent me, and hast loved them, as thou hast loved me" (John 17:23).

A. In Jesus' prayer, He recognized God's love for His disciples. God loves us too. He sent His Son Jesus Christ to die for our sins (John 3:16).

B. Today, mothers may forsake their own children. Husbands and wives may separate. But God's love is constant and dependable.

II. E-nables His Own

"I will strengthen thee; yea, I will help thee" (Isa. 41:10).

A. Many Christians do not succeed in doing God's work because they do not trust Him for a daily touch.

B. The apostle Paul said, "I can do all things through Christ which strengtheneth me" (Phil. 4:13).

III. A-ccepts His Own

"And him that cometh to me I will in no wise cast out" (John 6:37).

A. Christians may be tempted to wonder if God's presence and acceptance will continue when the chips are down.

B. In spite of failures and ill health, Jesus never fails. He is "the same yesterday, and today, and for ever" (Heb. 13:8).

IV. D-irects His Own

"When he, the Spirit of truth, is come, he will guide you into all truth" (John 16:13).

A. We must surrender to the will of the Holy Spirit and trust Him for direction. We are unable to make life's journey alone—safely.

B. The wise man said, "In all thy ways acknowledge him, and he shall direct thy paths" (Prov. 3:6).

V. S-ecures His Own

"For I the LORD thy God will hold thy right hand, saying unto thee, Fear not; I will help thee" (Isa. 41:13).

A. Millions are seeking security in houses and lands, silver and gold. They fail to find it.

B. Real and lasting security is found in God's presence, promises, power, and purpose (Phil. 4:19).

25

Victory Through Christ

"But thanks be to God which giveth us the victory through our Lord Jesus Christ" (I Cor. 15:57).

Christ gives victory to Christians because He . . .

I. Demands Faith

"This is the victory that overcometh the world, even our faith" (I John 5:4).

A. Many people lack victory because they do not exercise their faith enough. They depend too much on feelings, emotions, and works.

B. "Not of works, lest any man should boast" (Eph. 2:9). To increase in faith we must use what we have. Plant our seed of faith. Let it grow. And it will bring forth fruit, giving victory through Christ.

II. Dispels Fear

". . . my peace I give unto you. . . . Let not your heart be troubled, neither let it be afraid" (John 14:27).

A. Today's world is a place of fear. Millions are afraid of the destruction and devastation that is taking place.

B. Christians need not be afraid. They are safe in Christ. God's Word declares, "Fear thou not; for I am with thee" (Isa. 41:10). The Holy Spirit brings victory through Christ to God's trusting people.

III. Diminishes Frustration

"These things I have spoken unto you, that in me ye might have peace" (John 16:33).

A. Many Christians are frustrated. They are overly busy with their personal pursuits and possessions and fail to make and take time for God.

B. Victory through Christ comes to those who give God first place. "But seek ye first the kingdom of God, and his righteousness; and all these things shall be added unto you" (Matt. 6:33).

IV. Directs the Future

"When he, the Spirit of truth, is come, he will guide you into all truth . . . and he will show you things to come" (John 16:13).

A. Some Christians fail to seek the guidance of the Holy Spirit. They also lack victory through Christ.

B. Those who are led by God in this life will be with Him in the life to come. They enjoy victory through Christ now and also eternally (I Cor. 15:57).

26

Waiting on the Lord

"Wait on the LORD: be of good courage, and he shall strengthen thine heart: wait, I say, on the LORD" (Ps. 27:14).

When it comes to waiting on the Lord, many Christians are remiss. They are too busy coping with the pressures of life.

I. Be Patient While Waiting

"Wait on the LORD" (Ps. 27:14).

A. Many Christians are impatient. We want things to happen at their appointed time.

B. If things don't happen according to our plans and desires, we may blame others—or even God.

C. We must be patient while waiting. God's timing is always best. He is never too early or too late (Luke 21:19).

II. Be Positive While Waiting

"Be of good courage . . ." (Ps. 27:14).

A. Some Christians become discouraged and negative when they have to wait.

B. Waiting can be difficult at times but we must continue to look for the good, not the bad (Phil. 4:8).

C. We must be positive while waiting on the Lord. He knows what is best for us and how and when to bring it to pass.

III. Be Productive While Waiting

". . . and he shall strengthen thine heart" (Ps. 27:14).

A. Someone has said, "The secret of patience is doing something else in the meantime."

B. Many Christians lack strength to be productive. They try to do everything in their own power and fail.

C. We must have God's infinite power to help us. Finite
    strength is insufficient. God has promised strength to those
    who wait on Him. We can be productive while waiting (Isa.
    40:31).

IV. Be Persistent in Waiting

"Wait, I say, on the LORD" (Ps. 27:14).

A. The psalmist persistently admonished us to "wait on the
    Lord."

B. We must persist in waiting on the Lord. In our busy world
    many of us are too involved with personal interests. We fail
    to "wait on the Lord."

27

Win over Your Problems

"Nay, in all these things we are more than conquerors through him that loved us" (Rom. 8:37).

Everyone has problems. Here are some ways to solve them:

I. Find out the Facts

"And ye shall know the truth, and the truth shall make you free" (John 8:32).

A. Many people fail to find out the facts about their problems. They live with suspicion and speculation.

B. The first step to solving our problems is to know the truth—get all the facts. The promise is: "The truth shall make you free" (John 8:32).

C. The truth takes the guesswork out of our problems and sets us free from prejudice and thus helps us to solve them.

II. Face Them Fearlessly

"Fear thou not; for I am with thee" (Isa. 41:10).

A. On many occasions God admonished His people not to be afraid. When God is for us, who can be against us? (Rom. 8:31).

B. Christians should face their problems without fear. When we bravely look at all the facts, our problems will begin to fade.

C. Most of the things we worry about never happen. We should trust God for the results.

III. Forgive Others Freely

"But if ye forgive not men their trespasses, neither will your Father forgive your trespasses" (Matt. 6:15).

A. Some people fail to solve their problems because they do not truly forgive. They cling to resentments.
B. Forgiveness frees us from guilt. Jesus said, "If ye forgive men their trespasses, your heavenly Father will also forgive you" (Matt. 6:14).
C. Genuine forgiveness is a great problem-solver. We must forgive others freely. If we do, God will forgive us.

IV. Fortify Your Faith

"And this is the victory that overcometh the world, even our faith" (I John 5:4).

A. Many Christians do not have victory over their problems because they lack faith.
B. Faith is most important. The apostles realized their need of more faith. They prayed, "Lord, increase our faith" (Luke 17:5).

28

Words that Are Needed Today

"A word fitly spoken is like apples of gold in pictures of silver"
(Prov. 25:11).

In today's society, careless words are often spoken. Words that are needed today are . . .

I. Words of Cheer
"A merry heart doeth good like a medicine" (Prov. 17:22).
A. Our world is filled with sadness. People take themselves too seriously. Most of the news is about the bad things that happen.
B. Words of cheer are needed. Cheerful words help give a right perspective both to those who give them and to those who receive them.
C. Let us discover the power of words of cheer and use them more generously (Prov. 15:13).

II. Words of Comfort
". . . comfort them which are in any trouble . . ." (II Cor. 1:4).
A. Violence and wars have brought sorrow and bereavement to the lives of millions. Our world is a place of discouragement and discomfort.
B. Words of comfort are needed. Suffering is eased by comforting words. Let us comfort someone today.
C. When we comfort others, the Lord comforts us in return. "Who comforteth us in all our tribulation . . ." (II Cor. 1:4).

III. Words of Compassion
". . . having compassion one of another, love as brethren . . ."
(I Peter 3:8).

A. Jesus had great compassion on the sick, suffering, and sinful of His day. We must have compassion on others too (Matt. 9:36).

B. Compassion must come from the heart. It must reveal a sincere concern and understanding for the hurts and needs of others.

C. Words of compassion are needed. Let us speak them with a caring heart (I Peter 3:8).

IV. Words of Christian Love

"And be ye kind one to another, tenderhearted, forgiving one another . . ." (Eph. 4:32).

A. Words of hatred and strife are prevalent in today's society. Words of Christian love are needed.

B. The scriptures admonish us to "be kindly affectioned one to another with brotherly love" (Rom. 12:10).